Living A More
Me fe

Living A More Meaningful Life

inderjit kaur

PARTRIDGE

A Penguin Company

Partridge books may be ordered through booksellers or by contacting:

Partridge India
Penguin Books India Pvt.Ltd
11, Community Centre, Panchsheel Park, New Delhi 110017
India
www.partridgepublishing.com
Phone: 000.800.10062.62

Authors Note

This life is full of love happiness joy and lots of prosperity.

We just need to strive a little harder to know the meaning to this life. It is a gift we are honoured tobe in this life.

There are many different types of people in this world some make you cry some make you more happy only because they know what sorrow means.

This is up to us to acquire more wisdom and do little from our side to this humanity and be graced and show gratitude towards the great God who entitled us to be born as human being.

Thank you God for giving me this life.

inderjit kaur.
9th of august 2013.
Mumbai.

Thought

People are capable at any time in their lives of doing what they dream of.

(Paulo Coelho)

'OM SAI RAM'

Dedicated . . .

I DEDICATE THIS BOOK TO THE GREAT SHIRDI SAI
RAM MY GURU MY GUIDE . . .

AND

My departed papaji . . . Jaswant Singh Hira . . .

Also to my lovely SON'S Mandeep and Arjun . . .

CONTENTS

Acknowledgements

My deepest gratitude to Simarjit for inspiring me to write. I dedicate my cover page to you.

To Bhavini pancholi for always being a strength to me.

To Vaidehi karkhanis for boosting my morale and for being my friend.

To my lovely sons Mandeep and Arjun for motivating me always.

To dr. Priyanka sara for being so supportive all the times.

To my mother who bravely fought with cancer bless us all.

To all my sisters and my elder brother Kuldeep singh hira who is my philosopher, my guide, thank you all.

To all my other friends who truly believed in me aparna naidu, joan rocha, namrata kotian and all of my friends.

Last but not the least Farrina Gailey and Ann Minoza from partridge publishing house and the entire team of the partridge publishing house for being so cooperative humble and kind.

I hope you all get to know a little more of life from my book and take a small step forward in this beautiful life . . . keep smiling enjoy reading. Take care.

1

Life is Hard—BUT not Impossible . . . .

There is something always beautiful that has been stored for all of us every day in our life. The moment is indeed spectacular when we feel the bliss which is the centre core of ourselves deep within. It is of truth it is of love it is of zest for the life—there is no guilt here there is no fear here there is no darkness here is just splendid atmosphere a pure fulfillment and is just pure contented blessed soul.

To live is to love and be really thoughtful for the enlighten that opens us new doors to see how much life means to us and how can we give more meanings to our life . . . we live we love we care we are concerned for all that is surrounding us except ourselves . . . so why not to start loving and caring more first our life our pure blessed life . . . so that it shadows our pure thoughts around and we spread happiness in our environment first, then see the simultaneous changes that make our life more reasonable to live in.

One of the greatest mistakes many of us do is that we feel dejected very soon for small failures in life, we feel helpless for small losses, for small reasons . . . . we start feeling sorry for ourselves and others too. We get occupied with the thoughts; ". . . can I, i won't, was it, it won't, what, when, where how . . . ? Thus we indulge in killing the most precious and most valuable time in refining and defining only negative impulsions.

These small factors do ruin the positivity of the atmosphere also impact directly on us. Forcing us to come out with the statements like "life is hard . . . .—It is not great, not fair". Once we bypass or overlook or just ignore this small little effect of negativity or the word itself NO we can really understand the real meaning of this blissful life . . . it would not be hard as such—as it is always possible to revive all again.

We need to understand and believe the clear and clean perfection and the meaning to make ourselves accept the very fact—"Life is Hard—But not impossible". Slowly we tend to realize perhaps its hard but not intended to be making a bigger difference still it's possible: Thus the small negative thought when born itself is demolished by the more strong active and living process YES.

Every thing can't be perfect. Everyone has a unique way to look into the aspects of the life Portrayals in the given time . . . some overlook the problems some let it go some flow along with it . . . but by simply accepting the thought process as it is born, reminding yourself that "it is okay, I can deal with the challenges—finding all suitable opportunities in all odds: and that I can still make it" perhaps we all can make our life more meaningful . . . let me explain in much simpler way—

One day I got a chance to witness an awesome experience which elevated my understanding towards inner strength in a more defining way. A small child aged five getting himself all set to get admitted for the skates class. Initially he is very much excited to experience something that is very new and interesting his feelings are high before going to the class he tries at his home to get himself comfortably placed in the skates, but as soon as he tried to get up after fixing the laces he gets rolled down now because this is for the first time the thought process indulges him to try one more time . . . as he himself is enthusiastic in putting more efforts to learn something more he decides to try one more time, but again he is rolled down . . . this happens for four five times and at this stage he starts getting annoyed. Now what? The small little boy gets fed up he just manages to come out of those skates and sits in a very low state of mind. At this time comes the great help . . . this is observed by his mother she approaches him to make him comfort makes him understand what mistake he was doing, now here the Little child missed the thrust required to pull up and swipe the skates, which the mother tries to Make him to understand that he can't let it go before trying it once again in an different way . . . she motivates him, he gets all the courage again and this time he is skating smoothly and indeed enjoying the ride even before he has joined in for the first session of his class.

Thus we need to search in a more different way, if we need to come out of our problems.

When we find the problems hard we need to search wider angle hopefully we can get a better view also the solution, that was just missing earlier . . . thus in hard times we feel very much failed from inside But as we overcome the thought and recognize that life is hard but not at all impossible life does wonders . . .

Keep overcoming your negative thoughts as soon as they are born. Keep smiling and keep moving in life.

2

Feel the simple line—
life is OKAY . . .

One small crack does not mean that you are broken into pieces it may only symbolize that you were on a tough test but you did not fall apart inspite of unwanted odds; Great things emerge when we tend to get up after we fall . . . then we dust off and gather up ourself holding our life with immense courage and determination.

All cannot be perfect. Seeking perfection everywhere gives rise to more conflicts with our inner soul. we tend to gear up for an unwinning battle and get engaged in searching perfections; thus end up with dissatisfactions and discontentments in ourselves. Sometimes we spend and invest our most valuable period of our life getting perfections and get the things work according to our convenience. Sometimes we do that deliberately as a line of act because we feel we should fit in the place . . . but this is not at all necessary. we can live the way we feel more beautiful and contented inside and try to make ourselves serene with the life rather than seeking perfections outside.

When we focus more on imperfections we get a chance to travel beyond our goals and look above into more broader perspectives in life we can thus gather all the imperfections and make it placed in perfection. You can agree to simple line—that life is good ;and we should enjoy and appreciate the things where they are lined. Instead of falling down the habit line to put all in perfections just start insisting your ownselves that let the things be placed where they are meant for, remind yourselves its perfectly fine, problems are just absence of the required solutions at that point. No one can notice your tears no one can notice your pain and sadness but you are always noticed in your mistakes.

Don't get upset or dejected with people or the situations around you they both remain where they are unless you react. First step to be happy is believing in yourself rest all follows with you by default . . . Share joy and happiness get perfections in being more happy and cheerful, flake a smile that's the best remedy to overcome even the tiny little unfair thought. This blends ourselves more with ourselves. Since all that we face in life good or bad makes us more aware with lessons and experiences why not learn from them all let it be perfect or imperfect, so embrace the truth appreciate all as life is okay in its contentment and not in excavating it unnecessarily, be graceful with yourselves, let the negative feelings come and go, do not bother to pick them up.

This strategy of dismissing the forceful thoughts that tends to seek life isn't perfect leads us to seek Perfections in imperfections while ignoring small issues side by side. we carry more love care affection In our heart because we made a place for it now. Since we are rich with what we have in our Heart not with what we carry in our pocket we feel more contented and deserve to live a more meaningful life. When we search simple things we get simplified we accumulate more to face the strong world out there . . . Because if we are strong satisfied inside we can stand to any thing. Believe in your selves start taking initiatives if you take small steps they can be the start point to your journey.

3

Our dreams do not come with expiry dates

Even as I write these lines I get positive vibes just because only a positive thought has been created in the mind. Thoughts created can be really propogated into its correct place and implemented into the need for which they were born. This thoughts come as our dreams as we always expect and are in constant search. dreams do not come with expiry dates its we who defragment our dreams with out even laying out its format or taking even a single initiatives many number of times. We just discard them into pieces for no reason . . .

When we live in this beautiful life we get numerous chances to learn more acquire more grow more from within some people aren't more inquisitive to understand the truth. As I write I see the green beauty of the nature outside the window. There shelters a big vast almond tree with numerous and thousands of round oval almond shaped leaves flickering over each other in urge of pure light air and rain drops quenching their thirst. This can be ordinary for many of us but if we pensively look we get the answer stored, before the monsoon coming with all its lavish rains its summer time in India also climate is humid and hot in Mumbai before the onset of monsoons. almost all the leaves are dried up or not on the nodes, but as soon the rains set in we get a chance to evidence sheer beauty of nature with all shades of possible greens everywhere. Now this particular almond tree has multiple leaves from one single node when I see them in the morning I get the thought they are actually urging for this life they dare to dream more every day the need to dream does not set them back because many other leaves are in process to rise out . . .

Perhaps if it is dark once that does not mean there is no light. things keep on delaying there can be various factors associated but this does not mean those thing will never happen again in your life. We can dream at any age we are set in to, we can get associated with our thoughts lay them out format them proof read them finally implement them nothing is ever late. When actually we determine ourselves to stand firm against all the odds it becomes very easy to move up to our destined path. Once we are determined we can set our goals to achieve but if we are least prepared and due to some setback our dreams fail don't get upset. Giving back your goal because of a single setback is same like giving up your ride on the bicycle whose one tier goes flat and you just through it down that doesn't happen ever. We put our efforts to pump in the air in the flat tier and rejoin our ride and reach the path we were moving earlier.

Similarly understanding the potentials stored in you, You can create many opportunities also all the probable possibilities—don't ever bury your dreams because you were unsuccessful for the first time dare to dream more each day.

Work on it right through all your efficiency pure dedications try to be more compassionate be devoted then see the magic of your proposed dreams as they never expire. At any point of your life you can accumulate and reconstruct all your resources to achieve your target and fulfill the success lined up after every dream coming true. We got to travel through all our dark fears if we have to jump in the better and more meaningful version of such a beautiful life.

Hence I always recommend start dreaming framing formatting and implementing your own destiny just now. You are the one who can colour it with all the possible vibrant colours you want . . . Since dreams do not come with any of the mentioned dates in the calendar to get expired. keep smiling keep inspiring yourself and others too . . . .

4

Make place for yourself—

Each day may not be good but there is something good in every day. You try all hard also put enormous strength to execute your ideas to keep the show running but even then as you try to make things right there will be some people who will find reasons to make it seem wrong. So, Next what, rejection You go deep shattered feel low . . . this scenario may be at your house may be with your children at your workplace with your co—workers or your spouse . . . disapprovals break us down. You get frustrated with all the contradictions arising in your atmosphere ending up giving rise to more complex phases which we do not want to go through.

Every stage we get to accept the real challenge. We can't live in illusions we need to know the power of ourselves first. Where we are standing in life and we need to see what lies ahead The best stories come out of our struggles from our stormy days from our times when we went through rejections . . . just take a deep breath and soften your response.

Learn to open your heart amidst all the difficulties you will find the things that were bothering you get reclaimed into calmness because you did not over react and did not show equal oppositions, other wise things would have fallen apart. You should deepen your views and broaden your perspectives not by surrendering in difficult times but Reminding yourself that: "it is okay rejections, no issues I got one more chance to get approved and I am going to make it this time"

The spark of success is somewhere hidden in your failures itself, keep trying and stand again firmly, let the storm pass away. Just don't give up. I have never seen anything lasting forever even the heavy storms just pass away in some time. If you understand this you can revive one more time the trust in this life. Take time for yourself place yourself first in the line if you are settled with yourself then only you can settle all the external accounts of relations that need constant nurturing no matter what. There is much room for your life save it for all those good hearts those who really deserve to be in there, save them for good memories remember you are some ones smile, mend the fences which are broken or cracked we need to build bridges in relations not walls. Forgive people often let the toxic grudges wash away so that your body gets pure soul to reside in.

Now when you are done with all yourself placed in a place just move a little further no need to stand and get stagnant, all things around us keep in moving making us understand that when we stand at one place for long, we get rusted and when we keep moving we keep growing and prospering more. Don't let the behaviour of others destroy you from in, be firm and determine be most of the time happy and cheerful.

This is your life start making your place now.

The director of our life is GOD gave toughest roles to his best players get yourself this compliment that god trusted you so you are put into this life. Next time you are in rejection don't give up make yourself placed in better angle from where the view to your problem almost gets diminished. Troubles make us strong and well prepared for tomorrow.

The path of life is filled with high and low curves we can never reach the destinations if we block ourselves for small issues just make a cool reminder every time you face rejection "I will try again one more time in a different way"

THUS MAKE PLACE FOR YOURSELF WHERE TO STAND AND MAKE ENOUGH SPACE SO THAT YOU CAN MOVE EASILY FORWARD . . . . KEEP SMILING KEEP INSPIRING . . . AND ADD MORE MEANINGS TO YOUR LIFE.

5

Every day is great . . . .

I usually learn a lot from our nature and our surroundings have you seen winds complaining of being tired and taking a break, it constantly flows irrespective of temperature, rains, humidity or even cold. I guess if they would have been whispering as it is too cold I am taking a break or its raining so I am unable to flow' but this is not the fact. Similarly I hear birds chirping early morning round the seasons let it be summer let it be winter let it be spring I never saw them quiet. they follow there fixed routines early risers early setters making best of all day wandering here and there in search of food water. They are constantly on the move.

Here the catch is of course birds strive hard to survive we get to learn so many things from them. we can also contribute to our life is and keep moving keep struggling and coming out every time we are in we should keep growing keep on taking chances no matter we do mistakes we learn from them we can prepare ourselves for a more harder life which can perhaps feel the most beautiful when we take it at ease. A bird sitting on a branch in heavy rains or stormy night is not afraid that the branch will break and he may fall down because here he believes and trusts his own WINGS more than anything else. We learn here that we need to believe in our POTENTIALS, as everyday has all the power to give unmatched and unending opportunities as every day is filled with equal potentials we need to excavate the very best to make that day as the greatest day of our life.

Thus even our smallest efforts can sustain if we start believing and taking every day as a special one. Every day gives us enormous amount of energy and opportunities that we can start exploring our dreams and strive hard to make them real. We got to believe with all our courage compassions and desires to explore our credentials. Don't be afraid to stand for what you believe. When we start believing we also implement and that's the first step to success even though you have to stand alone just go for it as every day has a potential of making best

Every day gives you a chance to be more enthusiastic. Every day gives you a chance to believe in yourself. Every day gives you a chance to visualize and imagine your great desires and trust your inner strength. Why not make the best of the given life and this day that you call today. And make it the special day.

Time is the more powerful and the most supreme according to me once it is gone it never returns back. There can't be any good reason enough for letting it go without making or initiating the urge of doing that which makes us happy and more contented more serene. There should be no good reason to waste a day given to us by the divine God. Simply rise to the challenges keep on adding more values to your proposals of being the very best human being. Never allow your dreams desires imaginations to get distorted to get tarnished or to get rusted just only because you are waiting for the perfect day to arrive.

Every single morning everyday has a tremendous amount of energy to recreate the very best of you. The happiness entirely depends on your thoughts, at the end of the day you can start focusing on what keeps you holding and let go what is tearing you apart. Get ready for the next supreme day which is on its way to embrace you . . . keep smiling and keep inspiring to revitalize the meaning to your life. Every day can assure you to help and take more desired actions to work on your goals with courage. Make more brilliant and well deserved decisions. Colour each day with your rewarded designations. Colour each day with your good deeds of humility. Thus recognize the power of each day.

True ignorance is not just absence of knowledge but it is when we refuse to acquire it. Your footsteps turn your walk into making of your road. The path is laid with all your efforts. Excavate the hidden potentials of each day live it up colour it cherish it and see how life is being so wonderful and becomes more meaningful to live in.

6

Oceans of life are stormy and windy—we can't change directions of wind but we can change our sails.

Life itself is inarticulate to be categorize in a particular format. Challenges are inevitable we get into hurdles problems we grow through them we learn from them some time s we are rolled back some times we chase then we are pushed back we get punches that's clear by now that life does not have a smooth sail. The journey of life is occupied with hard and smooth path.

We have to indulge with factual proximity that we got to move in harmony and garnish our stormy oceans in life with much more inner abilities.

Winds may flow very strong circumstances may be very heart breaking and frustrating we may be facing disapproval we may be in dilemma—eventually we are jeopardized we got to be pragmatic sometimes.

We got to restrain ourselves in devastating conceptions . . .

"If I have to strategically redefine this storms of life I would rather put great deal of indulging first that hard times come and go we can't change directions of the winds in storms but we can change or re-direct our sails in the ocean of the life. In a nutshell I must relocate myself one step further even if I am in deep struggle and make the challenge as a test to myself now I don't need approvals of others. I have to search in my path how I am going to sustain from the challenges."

Instead of being very critical over a situation try to be more hopeful and tolerate the situation proactively . . . nestled it with all your great efforts and embrace it gently . . . try to retrieve if possible or change the directions and may be you get a better view or get to understand the solution for the challenge when you change your own view.

Now with your simple understanding and clear focused intentions wonderful things start happening. you will try and understand more with those whom you interact you will start loving your own inbuilt potentials you start loving your positive enhancing behaviour now. You feel much rejuvenated because the stormy oceans have passed away as you decided to change your sail and got a probable reasoning and solution to your situation which you were not able to see earlier.

The best place to find a helping hand is your own arm always trust yourself first bring the changes in you and the surrounding automatically changes and follows you.

The simple technique to some problems or situations is just to ignore and come out of that place as that time you may not be prepared to visualize the rise cause effect of the problem because problems are blended with many other factors too.

Sometimes we have to wait patiently and that ability while you are waiting proves to do wonders.

Yes we sometimes do mistakes life does not come in instructions and life indeed moves very fast too. people are really capable to live in their dreams at any given time of life period only if they change their perspective to more positive directions. when we have to step in more better phase and more better versions of our life we need to walk through all our uncertain aspects we got to walk through all our fears of that we may fail no we got to overcome that basic line from our mind.

Sometimes we are surrounded with more negative vibes we may have to be with them and we may feel lonely or depressed but we can all overcome this by keeping yourself engaged with those who make you more happy. keep yourself more who inspire you motivate you believe in you. sometimes it requires us to break to know what we are made up of. Still we can recollect reconstruct our path again it's never late.

Pains just don't show up in your life for no reasons they are the signs that you got to understand that some things are needed to be changed. We got to craft clean ourselves from within to regain our self one more time to be in harmony with our esteem. Small minds can't comprehend big spirits for to be great we need to willingly be hated mocked misunderstood it does not elevates more than that. When we feel deeply contented inside all this doesn't matter much.

Never let someone create an opinion for you that's you who can define yourself more of you so that others know you are in and that your amazing amplified magnitude to represent yourself more confidently changes the whole scene more positively.

If you don't know your worth and your value others may expect and under define you below your personality and they may formulate calculate you to be a person who you are not. And when you define more of you everyone accepts it and you feel and realize that the distance that you have been travelling when you look back was not a waste.

This amazing magnitude to self indulging makes you a strong person who you deserve to be and hence leaving a more meaningful life as it is said we can't change or control how the things happen but we can certainly change ourselves and control the way how to react at them. When we understand this and we don't allow our wounds to transform us into someone we are not we are really in a stage where we live a more blessed and beautiful life.

Be blessed keep smiling . . . .

7

Your words have the power use them wisely

It is very important to realize the effect of our mental dynamics. The close interceptions the close dissections and the close intersections of our thoughts that arise give rise to words, when we see good when we feel good when we hear good we inculcate and feed good positive thoughts which comes as pleasant words but when we feel depressed or we hear something that we can't absorb also when we see something that is not pleasant to our eyes we go deep down in our thoughts which keep on multiplying resulting into some unpleasant words which actually we did not intend to even say. This all is mental dynamics and once we rise beyond this parameters we can control what we should feed in and what we should not to make our life more meaningfully applicable to the society where we live in.

Whenever we think or listen or see we get engaged in thought process and this thoughts either intersect each other or these thoughts dissect each other. Thus it is very essential to be aware of what actually we are going to process and what will be the outcome when we put out them in words. this is applicable in all stages of life and all segments of our social behavior. when we are dealing with our family when we are in interaction with our sub ordinates or even our boss also our near and dear one's words which are out from our thought process via our mouth do not find a way back ever again. We got to be selective and very much concerned for what we need to feed in as whenever we are about to start a conversation or whenever we are reading or even when we receive a phone call we prepare instantly to reply and give our verdict we are more prepared to answer back most of the time.

Listening visualizing creating all this process is continuous and words are lined up our words are so powerful once we start emphasizing it more it starts giving result immediately let me give a small instance to this. When we say hello with a cheerful smile on our face even to a stranger the first impact we see on the strangers face he would immediately first smile even reply you hello within fraction's of second then probably when you cross each other away he may even think do I know him? Thus your face value adds up to your conversations along with your words which you say. Similarly if we try to express in anger and we say even a small word in anguish, so let the word be to your spouse or your little angel as 'do not disturb me' You know within fractions of second the little hearts respond in form of tears. That's the power of your words now imagine if you would have used thousands of the words in categorically good or bad till now in your life time, what impact they would have made to your surroundings your family your friends your loved ones and above all yourself we are in guilt if we unintentionally hurt someone that's the power of your words.

An excellent and an easier way to define what we think or starting a conversation even when you take a call is just be quiet for some time before you speak.

This strategy is rather more easy then to carry the guilt inside forever if you had unintentionally hurted someone with your words isn't it. this works more effectively and is rather more fulfilling and creating more trusted thoughts that would make you serene you become more gentle in your talks resulting in your atmosphere changing instantly and you get the desired results. a sound and gentle approach in your behavior is willingly and satisfied and accepted in all segments and all phases of our life. This will only happen when we safe guard our thought process and generate pleasant words which add meaning to live in this beautiful life.

We need to first understand the conversation rather than what we feel about it at that instance jumping in and interrupting a communication results into unwanted and unwelomed thoughts which are unprocessed unmatched to our persona we can imagine once they are out without filtering process what a clog and block they would be making of your personality in the minds of the ones with whom you interact daily number of times just think about it . . . it is very necessary to understand that when someone is interacting with you in form of a call in form of a message or in form of face to face conversation does believe in you got to be more responsible here as you were trusted by someone hence selected to be heard.

We got to be effective listeners we got to be more calm in responding this is the most simplest way to avoid many of such arguments and many unsolved problems. Many of us fight literally using tons of words involving ourselves in an unbalanced act of wasting the mental potential energy which could have been used to make something more constructive that would have added colors and memories to be cherished. Tiny dis agreements are stretched into life time battles of ego due to raised pitch of unpleasing words which are actually not at all required as we are in most wonderful creations by the god into mankind as this only results in hurting our souls.

Instead be always graceful at yourself also be grateful at your heart forgive very soon often take a deep breath before speaking and completely listening what was told to you it requires deep immense practice to be very calm these days but it is not so hard the power of your words can hit like a rock or soft like a dew drop in the hearts we need to be more under self study more relaxed more gentle more kind more happy more cheerful

Applying this definitely rise you above the level and you feel re born and you start liking and loving your life more and more adding meaning to your survival and adding meaning to your existence in human chain . . . be happy keep smiling enjoy reading . . .

8

*Relations do not come with price tags
conserve them forever—*

We are in this life surrounded with our precious relations they are blended from the time of our birth till we rest. we know they are there and we hardly feel doing something special for them we keep on post ponding, also in todays, life we take them for granted, we just are busy in our own world we forget to show any gratitude, grace, human bond let it be any relation family, friends, parents, work place, dear ones. We indeed are becoming more and more careless, we just keep on ignoring that they are present.

We can utilize every minute of the day for something good life has no remote or automation we got to standup and do it for ourselves try to be a distributor of love see you get it back multiplied Relations in all phase of our life are sweet like sugarcane. Being kind is more important and kindness is free we often tend to forget that. When we are set in our advanced ages we really keep on feeling the things we have missed or the things we could have managed to do in different way. we miss our parents one day when we see the empty chairs from the time of birth till we self evaluate ourselves that we are grown up and get distanced from them then too they are the one who just want you to be happy you are been cared in their hearts always you are been blessed each moments that is the definition of parents I may be listing very small amount of love perhaps they must have showed enormous did we returned that? Did we cared enough to see are they ok today did they had breakfast today no we are so busy in our busy work schedules but that would have taken perhaps a single minute just to hug your old mother while leaving for your office or just a phone call.

When we really want to seek inner peace try this excellent source of revitalizing yourself just spend few moments in remembering someone you love the most. See you bring down a smile on your face. once you make your mind how to start your day with a smile all follows up all your negativity is redirected into positive layers and you start distributing kindness love and affection. now the question is how does this matter to your surrounding of course we tend to spread love in the eyes of innocent beloved children who in return would be happy to receive happiness from you and prepare for the day ahead your spouse indeed would be ready for the day that has stored with great zeal you yourself at work will be more dynamic and cheerful. Redirecting yourselves is not hard we can change so many life's around us just by simple gestures of showing how much you care for them how much they are needed just surprising your wife with a flower from your garden or even writing a simple note that u will be missing her throughout the day and tag it to her working place or just leaving a pleasing note in your children study show casing papa loves you a lot.

This small efforts for the relations flow a tremendous message to the hearts of the one who are with you then you see double the amount you start receiving this is more constructive way of rejuvenating again your relations together and binding them in one place of your heart. Maintaining relations is not just getting an certificate since we live in social society it's a lifetime effort to nurture our relations as they do not come in price tags we often know there values once we lose them.

It is as magical as we nurture a small plant with all our love care and affection the plant grows back and flourishes us to give flowers and fruits. Similarly our relations need to be nurtured, give that what you want to receive. Sometimes we only need someone, not to fix or do something in particular we need them just to let us feel we are cared supported. Being kind is more important begin your day with gratitude. The more we nurture our relations with love care and gratitude the bond becomes more strong and trustworthy.

We can always start taking care nestling them in our hearts from where they don't get disappeared and are chosen to remain forever Hence be careful with all your relations they add up vibrant color form of energies in your life hence we can cherish more rendering more towards care and love forever. Today will never come again encourage someone today take some time to care for them let your words heal not wound. Perfect maturity comes when we forgive others and understand their only situation and move forward forgive others as quick as you want to be forgiven by god. when we will be empty from inside then only we can stake new zones of life filled with eternal kindness love care affection making a meaning to be yourself and as a defined person who understands what a smile means

Keep smiling and be happy.

9

Believe in yourself first—first step to success

Sometimes we are reluctant to accept the unavoidable circumstances i am sure thoughts at this times are deceptive because we are lacking inner peace. Despite the struggles which are slashing us we got to understand that we need to be more compatible to the situation and also first with ourselves, then we can match and bond with our surrounding frequencies in more constructive way. Quiet often we say, "I knew this would happen I should have done something about it-"

Now we have missed trusting our own thought sometimes our inner voice is just what our subconscious thoughts are which actually work for all possible consequences which can erupt we are warned by our conscience but we let it go unattended most of the times. If we learn with patience to trust and listen our inner voice first we can overcome good many problems since I define problem is a problem because it is not according to the solution which I am looking for or the absence of solution at that particular time arises the problem. If problem is sublimed with the solution as itself the answer problems may not arise only problem is just absence of solution.

We say things, "I could have possibly done that long before".—but now the time is gone. We argue within ourselves as we have limited ourselves. When we set aside ourselves more in calm be alone from hectic schedules we can practice more listening ourselves. When we start trusting ourselves more we start believing ourselves more and when we believe in ourselves more we become confident of ourselves and at this point of life we do not require approvals and opinions of others for ourselves.

At this stage we are confident of our inner being we know where we are standing and where we are heading and which direction is best suited to us. Our thought s can be garnished with all the harmony once we start trusting and believing ourselves. This intuitions no matter take a long time but we find they are familiar to ourselves, when we be in ourselves motivating ourselves is acquired. When our intuitions start pouring in parallel to our thoughts we got to be paying more attentions to be in a reciprocal mode and how to respond. Probably we can get desired results.

When we start trusting and believing more of ourselves we get tuned thoughts from our mind and heart. this small efforts of self approval makes a greater change more in from within us making us more positive in our outlook and create more visions for the given set goal we start more agreeing with ourselves and more confidently implement our projects this makes us re discover ourselves can be more defining our enhanced personality refining our behaviour which make us stand and face all the win win situations smoothly . . .

When we master to listen more of our inner being we understand tiny little flaws more effectively we try to eradicate them more finely and we start to communicate more confidently getting the desired medals of life Hence when we feel our thoughts emerging just spare a moment with yourself.

Hence believing and listening ourselves more make us stand firm devoted in this roller coaster of life Adding more meaning to an reasonable understanding with ourselves adding more meaning to life itself

Keep smiling keep inspiring keep innovating keep listening more of you

10

Learn to appreciate others for their say

So many times in our daily core issues we come across many unwanted things or at unwanted timings that try to change the entire scenario of our routine. For instance, you are busy getting ready for work, office, school and all of a sudden you see that there is no water, no gas and you get upset as your routine gets spoilt and perhaps you start blowing out resulting in all the anger spreading out to your near and dear ones raising a black, negative block in their heads early morning. If in case, they also ask you to keep low then you end up becoming more aggressive.

So next time if in any hard case scenario you are in a fix and angry and if someone decides to correct you, just appreciate with a simple word "thank you". Because he/she managed to block the unnecessary energy that you would have let out. This enormous amount of energy could have been saved for the tasks of the rest of the day ahead. It is not necessary to be defensive always. Think about this.

Actually, the only real fact is that we should be corrected by someone and be grateful to that person to see the zeal of contentment in our inner being. So never get upset with your situation or people. Both are powerless until you react. Also, the less defensive you be, the more lovable will you be projecting yourself. As the saying goes, people who argue should not be corrected. They like to get upset and make other people upset. So be graceful and appreciate others who correct you. Most of the time just learn to say yes and become more calm towards all opinions. Just simply allow them on the position they stand. The joy of happiness is more overwhelming than the joy of winning battles of relationships that end up only because of ego. So the best way to more peaceful and meaningful would be to change the habit of trying to prove yourself right and stop corrective others all the time.

A big pot of water can be emptied if it has a small hole. Similarly, good strong relationships can be spoilt with small moments of anger, ego and doubts. So just stop your ego from creeping into your bonds and just let it go. Keep yourself calm by saying 'thank you' instead of being defensive. Spend your energy in building new ideas, new ways to live your life because lapse of judgment is not always the problem. Hence when we listen more to others when we appreciate what they want to say we get a chance to understand that little flaws that we may be not getting into notice may be if others say or help us to understand what they felt we should give them a fair chance to have their opinion.

Keep listening more keep understanding more keep appreciating others more and above all keep smiling and keep moving in life.

11

Scan and erase negative thoughts

I just wonder the power of our thoughts they can run so fast. We are just in its shadow always we can creep for some good also but sometimes they keep on multiplying the minus points running and we chase like anything

After a long day and all the household chaos finally we seek a peaceful sleep with a peaceful mind. but does it ever happens sometimes we wake in mid hours the sound sleep is broken un knowingly that our mind did not sleep it constantly kept us wake because we are engaged with thought that next morning something was to be done that thought feeded while we went to sleep kept in reviving itself popping out to break the sleep

The important mind capsize and you lost your sleep now since you are awake for sometime you start thinking all that are lined up in process though that was not required but we do that very often ending up thinking everything else but not the important thing that was lined up for the next day Innumerable thoughts start popping up have you ever imagined one thought gives rise to another and another to still another and yet making you wander in mid of night. Finally you end up frustrating getting upset with your life that you can't even have a sound sleep but you are stuck with your limitations you could have been probably sleeping but you are in thought process that are multiplying.

Now how to make this situation more favourable is quiet simple you yourself allowed the thought process to creep down your memory lane without putting a full stop. This could have been done. As soon you broke off from your sleep you know you had a point running in mind just go to your table search pen paper write it down take some water just jump back to sleep this is not going to be miracle you need a lot of practice to cool your mind and nothing is there which is not achieveable. Just remind yourself 'okay now I should sleep' Yes we can do this being more positive from within can set this for you. You got to stop the effect of thoughts right away at the arising point before it gets some momemtum. Stop yourself remind yourself : here I go again ". . . I should sleep now". Just walk back to your bed and just sleep.

As things happen we can't control them but we can always control how to react to the things this is applicable in all the unsettled phases in life we can of course control how to react to the situation though we can't control it to happen the way we react the things react and pop up. This life is so pure this body is supposed to be like a divine temple as our soul resides in it we need to be careful. We can immediately stop all the negative thoughts from arising negativity knocks the door that does not mean we should let it in. Let it be left un attended . . .

Sometimes we have to do many things lined up but at times we do not have much to do that's life Some times are hard sometimes are tricky sometimes we are bouncing back so because one thing did not work that does not mean we start entertaining all the negatives impact and block our mind we should not bother and allow that negative block to keep us bothering day n night . . . If someone starts demoralizing you for any reason may be at work place we can't react as it will multiply just be calm it is also a lesson everyone teaches us some lesson just don't let your thoughts to jump and play to rule the scene. Just keep on doing your best if sometimes we are unable to get success with part A, don't worry there are still 25 alphabets to try in more different way just don't start thinking negative about your failures all that happens makes us to learn and grow we got to be matured to understand this.

Ever since we strive hard in search of our goals and in search of our dreams believe me our dreams our goals also start their way finding us. Just be yourself set your goal start nurturing with all your caliber isn't it more positive way to erase negative thoughts which popup

Be with those who often make you happy and cheerful this also is the important part of life the more we are in negative shadows we are influenced and get its impact too. Be with those who made you see the sun in dark clouds believe yourself be confident and see non of your thoughts will try to rule you. You can rule your thought, Since what defines us how we rise after falling down. Thus adding more of your being in your life the way you want and not the negativity just pure of yourself keep smiling keep moving with all the positive caliber.

12

Close some doors of pride and arrogance . . .
because they lead no where

We are surrounded by good many people, right from dusk to dawn we get a chance to inter act many of them. May be family relation friends—work place people. When we meet for the first time we tend to reflect and take only good exchange of talks, words, vocabulary, gestures, appraisals. We get affected to his or her appearance, and the outer look as a temporary personality reflection or these may be combination of good things and superficial outer look.

We have a tendency to cater up small issues we try to find up the cracks, and try to reform it we think we need to fix because its "I" who think it is not the way I want. But it is essential for the critics mindthat he or she should also think about those flaws detected and those remained undetected, these information detected may be not an issue for the person standing right in front of you.

After some times when things do not get improvised you begin to bring all into their attention. So the statement may be anything from, "I knew you do not like this", I knew you will be late," I knew you . . . . This ultimately reflects that you have started disliking many things in a person as person while he or she doesn't matter to such small issues.

This criticism, or you can say these negative remarks raise the alarm. When we find flaws in other it most of the time reflects the inner being of you itself.

These things needed to be taken more cautiously because our mind affects our mouth too. This kind of relationship cracks exponentially trials up leading to many misunderstandings. If we truly need to change our life first we should be prepare to change our mind persons who projects positive aspects always are seen to be moving.

While person who projects negative aspects are always seen struggling standing at the same place wandering which way to go.

Pride, bad attitude, arrogance these are temporarily crowned in our uppermost deck because actually we are far more small to be more expressive we need to maintain the habit of showing gratitude and not pride. These things are just like flat tire which can lead us nowhere. Being more graceful, courteous with relations can do wonder. As the deeply quoted words embark always in the history "relations are like plants they need to be nurtured regularly with Love, affection and care."

This arrogance, pride, attitude are some times more prominent in some ones behaviours. Some show sporadically but to be precise these lead only failures. We get tensed with these kinds of behaviour. So better we make a choice for a "Spectacular thresh hold of the beauty of life" and that let some doors which are full of pride, arrogance destructive, Pride be closed once for all—since if we do not close the door for showing people they recklessly recur again and again try to demoralize and defeat your inner being.

Keep understanding more of you and keep practicing more to be humble being arrogant leads only failures.

13

Don't Carry problem in head . . . use them under your feet as stepping stone

While we are walking we tend to walk in steps also do recollect when we, used to be toddlers we use to creep, crawl more with all our limbs That takes a process of exhibiting our needs to do something more and better.

Hence while we move in real life we got to face different forms, different sizes different amount different taste of problems perhaps true. So do we need to stop once we face them. No, we can either take it as a challenge & face it let it define our self, let it change our self learn through them potentially we explore the parameters of the problem. Pertaining to be small once gradually falling down as huge load on our small tiny brain. Now what can be done at this crucial phase of life just take it simple, make it as remarkable achievement. We can't reach in front until we leave behind what we carry & let go.

Making our minds prepared as this tend to be just temporary—Not a life time problem secondly prepare ourself that I am going to learn more perhaps through my problem are yet add feather in my cap. Ironically when we see problems in a different view we tend to lose its power and weight because we are prepared to face it all defined phrases. So let the problems come and go they make you grow make you to be more patient. They teach you to be more alert. Since last time you faced them now you are better prepared. Sometimes bad things happen in life so that we see good things which we haves saw before.

When its life there are struggles. When there are struggles, there are problems, when there are problems, there are lessons, when there are lessons, we get a chance to learn and we lead ourself to more wisdom and knowledge. This can be passed to our next generation. So next time you deal with any never ending saga of problem deal it with enthusiasm bring it close to heart. Retaining it to be your most rewarded teacher— write down the cause of problem, how did you face, how did you solve, because it was just temporary absence of solution at that particular moment, write it down for the next generation helping them out to learn different ways to deal with the so called problem as an creative master. Hence make the problems as your stepping stones to move forward make them your best master try to learn and grow from all your problems never carry them in your head keep them only in head to get best solutions.

So keep learning keep growing and keep smiling . . .

14

Rejoice the beauty of happiness its peerless

Life is indeed not very precise it does not come with instructions. We all tend to find it sometimes muzzy, hasty, there are obstacles, it pelts us down some times, it makes us ponder. Some people tend to live happy even in hard grey days some easily give up. It's pathetic that everyone cannot cater the different parameters.

If problems were prior known or pro conceived they would have been permuted clearly taken up each at a time. But this does not happen. We got to live life in balance of holding and letting go holding what makes you rejoice and letting go that cant be sorted out more meaningfully . . .

What gives you inner peace is very simple it can be just a smile also and letting go that realty can't be changed lets rejoice the beauty of being happy. This rejuvenates the heart and perforates all the things that makes us sad.

Each day we get older that is mandatory but growing up is an option do small things that rejoice make happy listening your favorite music. looking greenery out, flowers hearing birds chirp, no one loses anyone nor does anyone owns someone, it is just being too much worried or concerned, also sometimes brings selective sadness.

Just if our loved ones are gone very far away regard less due to time, or work in different country we tend to get low many times. Even this situation can be mesmerized that they are not very far away they are just sharing different room in the big house called earth.

Feelings emerged like waves it's just which we should choose to surf more or let it be there and it shall calm itself with time. While waiting we just show our ability of how we act in those crucial period.

We can't change each and everything happening but if have love happiness in our heart we can make small differences everyday—which can really change and matter a lot, small steps give rise to miles. Be grateful, be happy search for small happiness each day even if you have to look harder do not stretch a season of bad phase or a bad time into a season of life time. Nothing is supposed to be forever. Be cheerful.

When we are happy and cheerful we tend to make each and every little thing around us to rejoice, that's the beauty of life. We can be grateful and contented and always try to be happy, being happy is not a big deal. Make up this line, accept the feelings that low you, make your mind that even this too will pass away as the sunset. Happiness leads to help you grow towards more wisdom, and cheerful life—when we are happy just see the magic—it's contagious it send waves of positive vibes where you are and whom so ever in their surrounded by you. Happiness manages to find our solution when we are sad we need explanations . . .

The happiness of life depends more on qualities of your thoughts to be in nutshell.

At the end of the day try to focus what is tearing you apart what is holding you.

Try to write on paper and calmly get solution being happy is that simple, people often forget nowadays that kindness is free. So being kind is also a door that leads to immense happiness.

15

Erasers are made for who willingly accept mistake

When I see the road outside I see thousands of people, vehicles going thru and fro from morning till late night as if there search is endless just wandering so fast chasing behind the time. Now days our life is stress filled. we all are fixed in our routines we deal in our areas of work.

Sometimes we being not accepted or our thoughts are not willingly accepted. Since every one refuse to accept one other now days without knowing the truth behind the say Let it then be mother child conversation if mother points out the trendy or jazzy hair style the boy gets annoyed feels criticized wants to defend and now arises generation gaps talk which actually does not exists its matter of small changes required at both sides . . . the boy needs to look little reasonable instead of making fun of himself and mother needs to overlook sometimes giving him to understand why she insists him to change his funky hair style . . . thus eraser can be used if the boy willingly accepts to what is the reason that mother has raised the point on his funky hair style. so this goes in parallel When un acceptable comments are heard they are refuted in self defence many times. Negativity comes from all sides arising offensive and defensive talks to defuse this both should cooperate and walk one step forward. If the person looks it as an observation because the person who points is more concerned.

If this things are more accepted peacefully as good regards as take them more positively as helpful encouraging reviving steps this could be averted when we react to the statements to the person who tries to point out problems in us often we prove them to be right.

When you react to your critiscism you give them full marks for their assessments. Hence even if someone tries to point at you defines you more in all your flaws don't feel distressed take that as a challenge to accept Say a big thank you for helping you to understand more of you. When we become defensive in same dimensions to which it was targeted we become more upset impulsive just be calm at this point the reaction suppressed will also put zero effect on the person who if deliberately criticized you.

Sometimes people with harsh tongue are unable to sell honey and people with sweet tongue are successful to sell chillies too it's all matter of how you react to your circumstances and willingly accept to take eraser and rub of your minus points.

Accept your flaws that will polish you even smooth with brighter radiant personality. We can't change all at a time but step by step one at a time little efforts indulged deep inside to change ourselves can make altogether a bigger change. Some of the unwanted habits can be cut from the roots making you more grow from inside being more contented and adding more meaning to your life.

How many times do we accept willingly our flaws if we do we raise our levels high in our understanding reacting more maturely. What the observer has assessed can be taken up worked upon with great enthusiasm if you take it in spirits it's going to rediscover more plus points and enhancing your own aura . . . Be thankful instead of lashing out . . . We got to be willingly get mocked hated to be in great spirits because small minds cant incubate this we need to grow from within making more understanding with ourselves first Adding more meaning to be presented as living a wonderful life and peaceful soul . . .

Keep inspiring keep smiling keep living keep moving.

16

Collect the moments not the things

We are humans every day we got to simply match up with our life. we are not perfect. We go through many things. we grow, we rise we fall we learn we do mistakes, in a nutshell this life gives us enormous opportunities every day and so it is called the life.

We just got to look the solution when we are stuck in a different angle—we get more clear objectives. Thus life is wonderful we got to make each day each hour each moment special. No relation is a waste of time actually they teach us lessons that prepare us for the right one. you got to believe more in yourself first rather then the approvals of opinions of others.

Aim high keep going even of you are hurted today just keep moving. get going just don't sit on the runway quietly. you got to drive your own plane in new attitude with all the enthusiasm. No one is coming and going to push you forward to take a leap. You got to put efforts.

Cash resources money things are all very temporary what actually does matters are the happy serene moments which keep us motivated and alive even in our most critical hand times.

Don't let today's disappointment hinder in your tomorrow which can be prosperous full of energy motivation and life. Whole life we are chasing materialistic happiness thats just a substitute not requirement.

The real approach to seek inside we got to excavate the real happiness while searching the material objects outside. We got to collect all the happy moments we got to live energize each and every aspect of life This strings of happiness together do wonders we are contented from solitude we are contended from false take desires—collecting moments of lovely life is more easy then to collect things in life.

Just try to understand the real objectives behind the reality, actually it makes a lot of difference. We change from inside we see the surrounding a better place we love ourselves more hence we live happy more, hence the life becomes more meaningful to live in, everything has a beginning and also everything has an end too. All that is created will eventually disintegrate perhaps even a glass which is created but finally it will also shatter into pieces. when some things are not working according to our expectations we got to feel grateful and expect something to happen instead of getting immobilized. We know we are prepared—when a glass was created and it has to be eventually shattered into pieces—we can't expect more out of it.

We tend to be more pathetic with things we possess and are shattered when we lose them. perhaps when we broader our horizon and look out a different perspective we can make peace with the things where they are when we start to make our inner self aware and stand appreciating the simple tendencies we will feel the life as never before.

During course of life we tend to become more relaxed and less bothered of the things we collect. We deeply cherish the happiest moments which can bring smile on your face even in your deep loneliness.

17

Life is not about to win and loose

Life itself emphasies the meaning as existence—so true.

We are dealing every day with numerous stress we witness so many shades of life but still we manage to move further. If its life it has to be living we need to grow we need to flourish. If it is not moving if it is not growing if it is not flourishing that mean life is dead stale it becomes stagnant. But then too we categorize the definition of life in how to win certain battles that simultaneously emerge in the path—we never sublimate the pure strings attached to life from many scuffels we face. It is not even about losing where we ultimately subdue ourselves as if it's the end here. No life is how we react to the areas where we win and how we face the areas where we lose. We continuously indulge ourselves finding pinnacle view in every segment of our life rising and falling are inevitable what rises high has to come down one day that should not break our esteem.

We got to overcome this fear got to be prepared that it is okay we should keep on trying. Many times we fall down just because there may be something more hidden that we need to explore. While we are flowing with our imagination we can still ensure that we can somehow come out of this Once we come up to choose up the flaws and the thin lines more wisely, we can revive our inner strength, also we got to control ourselves at the time of success as we get carried away with our success and deliberately take ourselves granted without putting much effort for our next projects also are impulsive sometimes shadowing our over confidence, . . . these both areas are of concern how to deal with success and how to deal with failures Every day brings in something stored we need to strive more harder some times

Winning and losing is relevant but can't afford to change this criteria to render us with an unchanged stigma both the scenes we need to change ourselves. Thus we need to walk in confidence and that is far more better then running aimlessly, also we can't keep standing at one place in confused state that will make us rusted and we can miss all the opportunities for the life. We got to move finding all the corresponding avenues that are visible we need to find harder. Perhaps understanding more to react at a win and reacting more to a lost battle grows as we get more mature. Being determined being committed be in focused proves.

Reconcile our inner strength again recollect our inner enthusiasm again trying this is never late. Surrendering to the challenges does not work facing the challenges work, results may be different but participation is the must.

18

Your best teacher is your last mistake

Sometimes we get so upset trying to find logical reasoning when things go wrong. We are skeptical we don't want to accept the facts. We become vulnerable we are shattered when we come to know why the things went wrong. The ivory of such situation is we just flow back feel very low and try to be more pathetic of ourselves. Now the cause . . . cure . . . drama . . . , emotions all running high to the height of expanding un measurable waves—The remedy for such type of scenerio not very easy we submerged deep inside the pain agony loss or whatever the case is related. But still we got to come out of it and be serene. We got to enthuse ourselves to finesse the critical time. So what can be the last positive encroachment just take that last mistake where the things went wrong as your teacher.

Although all your surrounding may be in turbulence but you at the center should remain peaceful. It would be so nice to be calm & serene in middle of that chaos. You start breathing practice more of listening. The point here is that we can do it if we have made our mindset that it is okay & can learn through this and be well prepared to face anything more harder.

So when we don't react much other who are dependent get chance to enjoy the glory The truth is only keeping exercised about how to be more calm peaceful quiet even when all went wrong at the very first thrash of enigmatic bombardment and delocalizing it to spread it's chaos into bomb shell.

To incorporate this strategy is hard but not impossible. We got to make our mind set and change first. Sometimes we need to make peace with many imperfections. When we are engaged in where, how . . . when, what—went wrong we amplify the magnitude of dissatisfaction and discontentment.

The more we are inquisitive more damage we do to ourselves.

The strategy here is not ceasing either but building up more files of imperfection into a smooth curved path so that he can manage to walk the long way realizing that while there's a more better way to deal with it—last time it got drained off making your last mistake as your teacher . . . we master ourselves to be more creative more mobilizing the various Ideas that could be worked to the greatest potential despite of our fears inside . . . we manage to overcome and fulfill all that is coming more harder in the path of life with more proficiency more give in skills less distracted as last time putting more credibility to ourselves.

Next time you are down with mistakes failures stop ruining your self esteem simply with a counter statement that

"I learned from it that was great . . . . I can do even more better." Hence you also save enormous amount of mental energy that can be simply used for more better assessment, more constructive judgments . . . and better appreciative perspectives. So be happy in stating "I learned my teacher is my last mistake Life I am grateful to you".

19

Acknowledge: be grateful to those who love you

It is always the struggles and hardships that brings out extra ordinary from something that just ordinary. Happiness is found by living your life every day. we have to take life as a gift not accept it and just stretch it for the sake of doing it we are indeed bonded with many relations from the time of our birth till we lay down sound in our grave. Did you bother to take a little time and show a little gratitude to the first hands who took you in your hand. We hardly do or think about this.

In our path of life we are stringed into numerous people some are close relations some are well wishes some are our co-workers some are our guide some are philosopher to our life. Some are very intimate thus this all relations are very precious take some time to show your gratitude towards them once a while. That keeps your relations nurtured and our relationship grows and flourishes more and more.

When we first inspire ourselves the persons, relatives, overall your surrounding gets inspired by you. You got to be more positive towards your approach in relations when we get inspired from inside our environment directly develops and propagates new avenues. Just knowing and understanding the relations is not enough we got to work on them life time. So that we can preserve them, cherish them and remain in a unreleased bond. when you distribute your part of love into small small care and affections like you just hug your child for no reason, even when we flake a smile that puts a positive vibe. This frequencies add up and does wonder to the small tender heart which fills with have so your little efforts can make small differences every time and which leads to a bigger change in a more effective way. Be grateful be thankful show you really care be good at your deeds love with all your heart. Always forgive often that will really make you at ease we just don't know what lies ahead. Why not to revive the present moment which is the truth into a memorable moment to cherish through out.

Learn to appreciate learn to understand more learn to be peaceful more these all add up more to enhance your heart which shall always be grateful to all its relations. The greatest gift you can ever give to someone you love is your time your concern your care for them. Everyone deserves to be felt special and being loved we are humans we are kind loving and caring in our thoughts. Beautiful things starts to happens once we transform our little habits and appreciate the presence of our loved ones.

Grateful hearts are always happy.

20

---

*Life has many ways of testing . . . .
Be prepared*

One of my favorite quotes remains, "Your best teacher is your last mistake."

No matter how much I strive hard every day, I willingly acquire to get more out of each mistake. When I seek more, I learn more, when I learn more, I grow more to be more patient and being patient is then fine quality of heart. Life is itself a very huge, vast school and all that we learn, acquire, perform, hold, grow, display and practice is all a part of curriculum. When you begin to look all your tests as a challenge, you begin to learn from it and grow. Life indeed puts us on test in many ways.

Sometimes we get surprises we are least prepared to accept the challenges, opportunities but time does not wait for anyone. This time is our real test, how we accept or reject the proposed challenge or how do we face the problem viewing it as a challenge, viewing it as an opportunity or viewing it as an unfair decision to be made.

Life sets us to test just to test how willingly we can cope, how willingly we accept the proposal that comes sometimes all of a sudden. Life tests how willingly we can change to ourselves to deal with forth laid issues. How we can make use of our potentials, how we make use of our resources that is patience and tolerance. We are sometimes fixed in dilemma where we get to either select one of the given opportunities. Or life tests us by proposing many things all at a time or by not happening at a given time. When we are fixed in a dilemma, just be calm. Try to find out the best solution. Try listening to your heart more occasionally. We listen that our mind runs and results more rapidly, the answer. But sometimes we do the mistake of making the wrong decision when we are facing a dilemma because we seek help of our mind which may be affected with small percentage of anger from other factors—When we are put to test, we can come out and get a chance to succeed-

We can still rise ourselves above the problems and challenges set as an opportunity to learn and grow. We feel the things are right only when we see all things are working perfectly. Many times when we are coping with our subordinate or our teenage children or at a workplace we often disagree to their statements or even vice versa, they may disagree to our statements.

Now rather than struggling and considering this disagreement into a big problem and a test, if we can change a little perspective here that's okay. I get a chance to understand them and learn from this one more chapter of my life.

You are just sorted out, you are put to test and you willingly accept it to go through and learn from it. We need to ask ourselves first why I find problems in these issues, why I can't see them in a different perspective. May be I can see a better view and also the solution.

If a teenage child is arguing for more funds, instead of a direct no, ask how he would be utilizing it. Try to talk to him/her with comfort telling your own teenage stories. How did you manage to get your own pocket money? Thus you try to make him understand the value of money; time also gives him/her a green test that he needs to be aware of his accounts too. He/she can't just keep wasting his/her money and time. Now see the result. Your teenage son or daughter openly discusses his heart and readily comes to you for their other problems seeking a better solution. If at that point when your teenage son asked you for some money and you would have just said a harsh 'no', an immense amount of negative energy might have passed between you too. The most sensitive part is that the bond between a child and a parent starts disintegrating.

Thus be prepared to face the tests our life lays down for us. They make us learn, they make us grow into more mature human beings and make us more socially responsible. They also make us believe that life has a perfect meaning. We just have to understand and live this life projecting ourselves as a better human being every time and contributing our bit in leaving a more meaningful life. Whenever we are tested by life, we are put in a dilemma. We have to be very responsible here. We have to listen to our hearts very closely.

Even right decisions taken in anger lead to wrong destinations, Sometimes success leads to ego killing the discipline. We have to remain more graceful in gratitude. Never try to cut the branch on which we sit. Success is not forever.

Sometimes a person who talks rudely cannot sell honey but a person who talks sweetly can sell pepper too. All the crowns are not made for our heads but we can certainly hope for some crowns to fit us. Be ready for any test by making life a better place to live in adding more meaning to life.

Keep moving, keep smiling.

21

No one can drive you crazy unless you give them the keys

Life has many ways of testing our patience persons will to face it—either some times nothing happening at all OR sometimes you will find everything happening all at once. You are getting ready for your work, and suddenly your friend calls for some life melodramas happening at his place. Now assuming the concern you try to give your, all possible solutions, suggestions also blocking your time, nerves, but mental stress at that of hour when you know you are getting late for you work gets more elevated. You know you are running behind your routine schedule and when you land at your workplace everyone starts troubling reasoning demanding you. Most of us get caught in such situation many times at work with our neighbor with our children. Even sometimes with those whom we do not know. Now the key is to understand the very basic outlook on life whether, that was required—if you would not here attempted to pick the cell your friend must had called somebody else.

This doesn't mean you are unhelpful you don't care for others or you don't bother such terrible situation arised simply you attended a call.

Your time, energy, your work priorities all are disturbed and reflect in day ahead. True ignorance is not absence of knowledge but refusal to acquire it.

The real happiness of your life directly depends on the qualities of your thoughts. We ponder in ocean of thoughts which can be really good or even bad. We need to practice to choose the parameters and receive the most splendor majestic thoughts to flourish. You got to revisit the purpose of your life it's time to re built again all that you have already lost. Stand in your own power it's your movement conquer your fears— you have greatness and potential to make it the best. If you believe in it with all your heart with all your might you can always make best of those perfect movements.

Nobody can make you crazy until you offer them the key to control your own little mind which actually survivor in your own body. Life is short to wonder what could have been. Don't let someone dim the light of your presence simply it's shining in their eyes.

Thus even if you are been disturbed by outer influences comments remarks don't let it get affected yourself you should be aware what to take in your brain what things are needed to be kept away from your mind heart., even if someone tries to drive you crazy or tries to make you lose your temper just do not show any attention. you should be wise enough to response.

Keep smiling.

22

Nestle your relations close to your heart . . .

When we actually understand each other there should be no place for misunderstandings . . . all relations need to follow this simple line but since there can be some kind of issues that always remain unsolved creates lots of differences in the relations. All relations need to be cared loved and treated more respectfully . . . the more we look upon our relations as our earned asset the more we can place them on closet to our hearts. When we get to understand that certain behavior changes are seen in our relations we need to understand that some things seek attention and need to be repaired immediately before the crack turns the figure of break.

We need to seek the reason behind the changes we got to understand the point of view start to explore the aspects others want to make clear may be we are not bothered enough but this can 't be done. We need to focus the core reasons why the things are not in smooth conditions as earlier life shows the Irony of sadness to know what is happiness life shows irony of being absent to know what is the Meaning to be present so just we need to look into this relations in a more understanding rather then taking them for granted.

Every relation has its place every position is very important if we know the real value of that relation We will never allow it to collapse down or afford to lose it . . . we can't make and break relations for the sake of fun this are needed to be handled more with love care and affection . . . be concerned for all those relations you hold parents, children work place, family. All relations have their simplicity and their own importance. We need to make all set in their respective place making them more meaningful and for being special purpose they are not here for the sake of just names. We need to add importance, and closely nestle them, nurture them with care love appreciation trust and all the goodness. Because we can't make and break relation every second, it takes years to make a strong relation to build trust but it need just a second to break. So be very careful to nestle all those relations in your life those remain very important for your life they add meaning to your life and also your presence your existence in life. Enjoy all the colours of the relations nestling them close in your heart.

Broken strings can always be reconstructed by just adding more of your kind and affectionate efforts. It is never late to be reborn again because life itself is very beautiful it keep us reminding us every evening that I am coming tomorrow do not lose the hope.

Keep trusting keep reviving keep nestling all the beautiful relation in close to your heart.

23

We all are different we are special

It is because we all are different we all are special. We are blessed with this life we should articulate our gratitude towards the divine lord to bless us with this spectacular wonderful life. When we look up upon the skies we should be filled with strength to keep moving as planets keep on moving they are never tired.

When we look ahead we should strengthens our vision as once we open our eyes and we can see what lies ahead, we just need to start preparing our walk that efforts we have to make. When we look back we should see our hearts filled with all gratitude to what we were blessed till now what we have achieved and what we walked so far to get more of positivity and building your hearts more strong for whatever comes ahead be prepared.

And when you look inside yourself you should seek patience peace persistence calmness contentment. Each day should be concluded immensely filled with more cheerful thoughts as we are special we are blessed in soul we reside in our body feel special feel happy feel good. This spreads happiness around you.

Blessings are bestowed every time responsibilities are shouldered upon us, because the God believes us, trusts us that we can cater with the given task perfectly he gives us all the strength to go through all our highs and lows of life.

Never we should blame anyone for our life. There are many good people who gave you immense reasons to be happy. Some people taught you great lessons and surged you with experiences and best people fostered great memories in you forever. So we got to learn from all.

Pray your eyes should see good so you do good, heart always forgive, mind that forgets that you were in hurt, just keep smiling hold back walk confidently don't worry about the speed but moving is must keep moving on in life . . .

Don't ever lose hope and faith every morning brings new hope and blessing.

Keep smiling be special feel that good from within, see the transformation, more you make yourself good been cared more you start loving this great beautiful life . . .

24

Six letters word—MOVE ON
—means a lot

You are not entitiled to any stigma or negative titles or remarks until unless you stop trying . . . Just overcome some small little tiny expressions—'if "can I, what if, and just change them into "I can. I will I shall I can . . . Keep climbing the steps with all the hopes alive—you get roses only when you go through the thorns.

Life is a very enlarged canvas we can paint it the way we want please do not wait for someone to paint it for you because there will be very few colors and you will be left with less options. God has provided you the canvas just pick up paints and brush and start to paint the canvas of your life . . . The road to success is already with so many tempting things that are good enough to break you sometimes they can block you deep down from our heart convincing you to give up . . . but you do not do that. keep moving the word MOVE ON is just very small has six letters but it emphasis the entire life in it.

MOVE ON

"MOTIVATION ONSET with VIBRANT ESTEEMS to an OPTIMIST NAVIGATOR . . ."

IF WE UNDERSTAND THE LINE THAT MOTIVATIONS ARE ALWAYS ONSET INTO VIBRANT COLOURS OR DIMENSIONS ONLY IF THE NAVIGATOR IS OPTIMIST HE CAN MANAGE TO MOVE ON IN LIFE . . .

This magnificient Euphoria of being in meaningful life is elated.

When our thoughts are more nurtured with motivational morale the Onus of variant versatile opportunities are laid down . . . . do not lose the hope keep moving in life all the avenues open automatically.

We need to be more mutable we need to remove the obstacles on the way and keep going we need to be more enthralling to align with the opportunities to keep on going towards our destinations we can't stand at one place we got to move ahead if we are failed in relations no need to stand and cry just keep moving if we do not let go past baggage of hurts pains failures how can we accommodate the new joyful memoirs be ready to get more aquainted to life keep on modulating yourself as time is in gather more of good virtues good deeds let good fortune settle in . . . keep the velocity going taking comfortable momemtum of life do not give up just move on . . .

Keep inspiring keep going keep smiling keep acquiring more happiness and keep on adding more meanings to your life . . .

25

Do not keep baggage of past: there will be no place for more happiness to get in otherwise . . .

Sometimes it is very important to understand what we hold in our heart. We can't let it fill with grudge and keep expecting new beginnings no that's not possible. Keeping grudge against someone like letting them rent in your mind forever and giving them access to disturb you as much as possible.

One day a teacher at high school made her children understand this in very different way she told them to bring some tomatoes to school in the bag as told by the teacher the children brought the tomatoes the next day the teacher told them in the last period of school that they have to bring the same tomatoes next day too this kept repeating until children started to complain that the bags have started stinking and they can't hold them anymore. so the teacher allowed them to discard those staled stinking tomatoes and told them to gather in assembly.

Now the teacher asked those students that were they able to get the important message in this. perhaps children could not give the answer so the teacher says "our life is very beautiful so we need to take lots of care to keep it lively peaceful radiant joyous every time when we have some pains inside the hearts or when we keep grudges against someone or if we do not forgive those who have hurted us our hearts our minds our souls get stinking the way tomatoes did we need to immediately discard this ill effects of negativity, we should forgive them as soon as we want God to forgive us. Thus it is very important to how long can u hold this pains grudges they need not to be resting in our hearts our body should have pure soul to be rested, for life to be cheerful."

So why should we hold such things for long those bad memories hurts pains start getting stale and start taking the place of positivity too our inner self too they may even transform you into someone you are not . . . so like you throw away that serves no longer a meaning but is staling stinking hurting your inner self should be discarded soon.

Do not carry baggage of past for long—or how you will make place for new things to come and get stored in your life as happiness, so the best remedy for this scene is to rejoice yourself by just throwing away bad memories and how can we live in more into act of survival by self indulging by self learning that "I can't carry with all that occupies me and keep me unhappy that makes me stale from inside that is leaving no place for my life to live"

Life is about all transformations for all change continuous process to grow in. A child grows into adult a seed to a plant to better life. We need to get transformed for something better. So start unloading old baggage of hate anger grudges hurt pain. Just let it go away with flow of time keep your heart fill with just pure thoughts happiness joy. And a urge to be in best living adding more meaning to your own life empty yourself from all these pains start travelling light . . . keep the radiance of life glowing inside you. This adds more purpose for us to be humans . . . so keep unloading pains and start loading just happiness . . . love . . . life . . .

26

Being contented in your space

Life comes as a gift every day in form of morning. We got to acknowledge this and be grateful to God for providing us one more day. I see people striving hard every day to get more and more all the materialistic things all the things that keep them in comfort though the person may be sleeping on an soft bed but he doesn't get a peaceful sleep. We try to accumulate more than our needs then we keep on worrying taking care of those things and never living our life we need to form a habit saying what I have is more than I deserve thank you oh God I see people sleeping on foot path I see people with no legs but I am thankful to god to give me this life thank you God that I can walk that I can hear that I can see Why can't we be happy and contented with what we have, instead of getting more greedy to get more of our bank balance.

The more I greed the more I am unsettled we need to search our inner self. The more I need, the more are my worries, isn't it. The more I get disguise as I don't get as expected this makes us more dejected . . . the less I have the less I am worried the more we are relaxed the more we are free and relax. Just see the under privileged people and then feel where you are there are people who sleep without food and water. Thanking god for everything he gave more than needed is the best prayer that we can offer. Once we start living contented with our own space we will no more be wandering here and there. When you give up your desires of getting more you expand your focus on self contented inner Peace . . . we can re create the thinking of self satisfaction rather than wishing more of things,

Be happy be gratified with what you have we start living more happier more cheerful more easy and smiling always. In life if we have less things lighter we feel we rise up feeling serene. enjoy the bliss of beautiful things around. And we start focusing on all positive aspects of relations more zest for life making us to be at peace with ourselves adding more meaning to our life . . . Being happy with what we have taking good care where we belong. Seeking happiness in our own small world and thanking the great god for this awesome life.

27

Be more creative in yourself
organize yourself.

I have seen people chasing life day and night, working more and more to earn even more and store more. Indirectly ruining their health and just adding all the hard incomes on medical bills. Whatever is earned is invested in medical emergencies finally the life ends up living up much for the core reason we are here is lost we never live our life.

If we try to organize ourselves more effectively more efficiently making time making a place for ourselves will be far more easy. We can work we can enjoy the little things we can work we can meditate we can do what we like the most we can cook we can take care of our little garden this all things can be well organized keeping you busy and above all giving peace of mind.

We need to take care of ourselves better we can understand our health our life better we can synchronize the routines and relaxing times which can work in harmony and give positive vibrant effects on our life. We can enjoy all the phases of life. We can give rest to our brain and in all our body organs get revitalize. Drinking more of water is one of the best thing we can do that makes a lot of difference.

Getting up early taking small sessions of garden walk or deep breathing makes you revived more energized for the whole day then making a list of things lined up for the day giving priorities to your work focusing on your fixed timings of breakfast lunch, this all together can drastically change and do a makeover of yourself from inside also your outer mind frame you start thinking more positive and start loving life you start believing more of yourself directly making more confidence in you.

Assigning some time for yourselves from your daily routine doing that what makes you little happy doing that what relaxes your mind then again you can join in your work this relaxing break after 4 hours of your work schedule is a must even let it be for a short period of ten to fifteen minutes just put on headphones enjoy tunes that you like most or just stroll in office garden or just sit quietly for some time this does wonders you are again fuelled and geared up for next 4 hours for your work.

Do not forget to drink water, at least we should make a habit of drinking 8-10 glasses of water every day this detoxifies our body energizing and you feel revived more active., and happy.

Spending quality time with your near and dear ones your children gives you immense pleasure . . . this happiness can't be measured on the scales, interacting with your friends once a while . . . this all add up to your persona, maintaining a diary of your medical checkup your important dates . . . calling your friends once a week writing down your stubborn habits trying to rectify as much as you can . . . so this small efforts to organize yourself add up an immense meaning to your life . . . I don't think it's a big deal to organize yourself its very good and successive step of being happy more contented it becomes a habit of being happy life becomes more innovative you learn more because you get more time as you are flourishing in happiness and ease . . . . so keep maintaining yourself health wise.

Keep smiling keep moving.

28

Forgive others that is very essential.

The simple and beautiful phrase is forgive others often and as soon as you want god to forgive you.

We need to understand that we have to make things simple we need to forgive those who hurt you sometime.

You can't hold the grudges it is like renting them in your brain so why not to just let go and move on.

Always pray that your eyes see that is the best and your ear hear that is good make your soul so pure that never loses faith so be humble and forgive forget while you are on the move of this enlightened life . . . raise your level into more pleasing thoughts make your mind occupied with all happy moments leave no room for negativity grudge hate anger. Just be clean pure and see the inner soul making all efforts to make you strong and always in joyful mood.

Mind is constantly generating thoughts if we do not forgive those who hurt you that means we are indirectly allowing them to punish us we are suffering from the guilt not they once we clear this block thought we are sorted out we feel light we are more free towards glory of our inner self which is pure truth . . .

A mind that stretches itself from low issues of anger hate grudges in to higher levels of forgiveness calmness contentment can never go back and fit in those early dimensions again because now it is lifted high filled with only pure love and the healing of true mystic powers of god . . . when we live in contentment we are always motivated from inside to live a more better life we feel rejuvenated, we are modulated into frames of successive happiness and we become optimist we start believing more of our self and we get the key to the lock which had stored dark blocks of pains sorrows you got from people once we start forgiving we also forget and we live more enlighted we resolute and start reviving the more meaningful things in life.

The metamorphosis from being low to more of yourself makes us grow from inner self we learn from all our failures too we learn from our achievements too we know our potentials, we gain self confidence our esteem starts elating into new height . . . so keep forgiving keep moving keep smiling.

29

Trust the creator more—truth prevails

The greatest advantage of the truth is it can't be hided under curtains can't be dismissed can't be defragmented as its truth always stand firm. We don't have to remember much if we tell truth. Truth gives you more inner strength and make things very easily. Confident walking is better than running in confusion. This means as simple as if you chase run with time aimlessly it is just waste but when you are focused determined filled with inner strength to achieve your goal that confidence is great going. Life is just like riding a bicycle to keep the balance we must keep going in confidence no matter you encountered failures don't give up make up your mind try it once again but keep moving.

The creator is very supreme he knows your potentials he knows you more sometimes he doesn't change the situations because he is trying to change your heart to get more prepared for the hard things with more of confidence.

Living on earth is a unique experience we are fortunate to be in this life, we get a trip round the sun every year isn't it great can't we start seeing things more positively to attain all the happiness. Every new day that comes brings all the great things happiness pleasure we need to strive a little harder to get all. paint the drawing of life with your prayers every morning see the magical effect you feel so enriched from within. Erase your mistakes just forgive all. Dip the brush with patience and colour yourlife all with colours. Be strong enough to let go be wise enough to wait very patiently for that is destined for you that you deserve . . . do not allow the struggles pains wounds transform you into a person you are not.

When the train is passing through the dark tunnel do you get up tear the ticket and jump out of the train probably no you won't do that—because you trust the driver you know now its dark because you are in a journey which is passing through darkness but still the train is moving isn't it. Similarly in the life when we pass our journey through darkness we go deep in distress sorrow feel helpless . . . so get up in your dark times too you can trust the driver of your life the supreme god trust him and keep moving in your darkness too just praying god that I know you are testing me I am your child please give me all the strength to go through this . . . see the magic happening you are transformed with all the strongest powers that you can face almost everything now so trust your creator . . . the divine god he blesses us always.

Life is full of all the beautiful things . . . soft sunrise and amazing sunset they always bring in a special strength and a special message, the rising sun says; "among all odd of darkness of night I never fail to rise . . . i rise to achieve . . . to spread light. I rise to reach all the dark corners of world. I give all the lights to keep the life starting all over again and again in continuation . . ." isn't it the best message that inspires us every morning filling us with a new hope always . . . and the sunset smilingly gives us this message "though I am tired of my voyage today I am settling in cool settling in to be calm for a while letting the moon also see you once a while don't be afraid I am not leaving you in total dark the hope of little light in form of twilight will be always left for you and I promise to come back soon stand again strong firmly reaching out for you no matter how tiring is it to be in fire all time I feel priceless by devoting you by showering my blessings as light and life on earth I get never tired but need a small break for a while but coming early in morning do not lose the hope". . . .

So it doesn't matter how you get knocked down in life what matters is how you rise again after falling down. So keep yourself always filled with great hopes this life is splendid. So live life and make it your best place. Keep smiling keep inspiring keep moving . . . be blessed.

30

Multitasking can't be good always

Sometimes we are very eager to complete all the things single handed we want to finish it off soon and many times we are unable to finish that as we are investing in many works at a time two or three is reasonable but doing multitasking can sometimes be dangerous.

I see a routine in most of the houses early morning mums preparing breakfast arranging books in the bags for children their uniforms spouse waiting for tea newspaper little kid out of bed crying for mum so many things lined up suddenly door bell rings mum manages to run and get the newspaper by the time she is in kitchen sandwiches are turned black milk over flowing from vessel just imagine the chaos so probably if each of the family member understand this and distribute certain work same things happen at work place do not underestimate or even overestimate just be in normal line of doing good work quality work confident walking is better than confused running imagine a single mind just piled up with or rather stacked with lots of work together we often get confused from where to start and how to complete.

Just relax be early riser start getting organized get the orientations complete some work in night itself like tell your kid to arrange timetable for himself this self doing habit will make him more confident other then he or she depending on you . . . working in timeslots without creating chaos let your spouse partner understand your pressure on work he should come willingly to be helping you in wee hours. Perhaps it will be more convenient you start being present in the work you are doing this applies at work place too if you are doing multitasking you are doing it for the sake of doing. You are not doing it with your presence of mind you can't concentrate to what you Are doing this results in your work been finished half done or without the desired results.

When you take one work at a time you are focused you are not distracted. This makes a great difference We need to understand the very essentials how to tackle things things can be done more efficiently and more interestingly you can decide more perfectly you are more positive and the things sorted out in better way so keep focusing on little things keep doing things more perfectly keep smiling keep moving in life adding more meaning to your perfect happy life.

31

Help others get the—blessings . . . .

Whole life human being strive hard to get himself established earn the perks get himself all the worldly comforts and chasing his dreams and always greedy to get more and more . . . .

Just imagine how we collectively keep on the journey as a continuous process that's good of course it results great but make us exhausted at the end of the day. There is no substitute for hard work but as and as we grow and go into the zone of success and comfort levels we fail to see from where we have started, do not let the achievements spoil you and make you run away from your roots. When we are busy collecting our baggage for thousands and thousands of years we often forget that the journey to which we are offered may be of few years only, why so we gather so much of materialistic comforts around us.

Greed is a never ending obsession in human race . . . we carry a lot we keep on expecting to get more and more often whole life we keep on getting best things for ourselves, and keep ourselves indulged into establishing ourselves and stand in our surrounding. To seek something more of importance that is name and fame. So when we shall live then, we are just wandering always seeking best that is all artificial temporary not real.

We got to make little efforts to look around ourselves . . . seek the blessings from those who need us to support them help them with their needs contributing to our society that adds an excellence behaviour to our life books, try helping out some mother who lost her only son in the war . . . seek to give happiness to a motherless child, try to give little happiness around yourselves to those who are under privileged try to share their sorrows and bring a smile on their faces and in return get the blessings . . .

Try helping little things those who need see the amount of happiness they get in all your little efforts they bless you from heart this gives us greater internal strength and happiness to relive our life . . . and this adds more meaning to your life as being a human . . . keep smiling keep helping keep getting in the blessings . . . .

32

Discover yourself . . . .

We know we are heading a very stressful life-we almost run along the needles of the clock.

We get ready for our work somehow manage to gulp breakfast take our bags and head for our office do we spare time to understand of ourselves which is the need of hour discovering our inner selves adding to it all the potentials we have, we need to find more of our qualities. This can be only achieved if we spare some time for ourselves during the week ends doing what we like the most, we are surprised to know our potentials as and as we get to know of ourselves.

The best part of this is we can get ourselves more motivated more prepared for the worst since we know how much can we with stand we can even manage to practice and make our self more strong more aquainted with the life and be well prepared for a better future and a meaningful life.

Being grateful being kind being more helpful mesmerizing all the inner qualities we have as an individuals we can work more on our flaws. Once we know what is stored in us. Getting up early seeing the sunrise makes you more confident more energized we get more of knowing the inner peace we are actually supposed to be, we unnecessary carry all the negative blocks and drain all the good qualities of ourselves.

We should keep best part of our lifes as momentos . . . keep smiling keep living gratefully.

33

Focus on little changes required

Time changes day changes into night seasons keep on changing change is constant natures unbind display.

What remains constant is the change. We get to learn from this that when we see something not working into the desired results or the pains or some things that remain as it is constantly needed to be changed. If we find certain aspects of life propelling even though that is not needed this has to be seen and considered properly. If we find some pains arising if we see some reluctance in our life we got to know something is needed to be changed. As we are different individuals but still we all need understanding that everyone deserves to be happy and live a peaceful life we got to create space for ourselves and also give them the place to flourish.

If we just focus on small little things that are needed to be changed this can do wonders. If you have a habit that irritates or creates a problem in the environment we need to focus on it soon. Suppose you like to watch some channels in television and at that same time some matches are relayed and someone in the family can't afford to go without seeing. Just don't be stubborn or try to be arrogant this times are very important to project yourself try to change a little, try and understand is this happening every time thus the clash of timings getting over the relations, just get alarms watch this very delicately.

You need to focus on that very willingly be courteous to your relations be very kind just understand the little requirements of your relations this little changes rectified do a lot of wonders. If you really care for others you got to put some efforts not just talk.

When my little son asked me once "Mom can I ask you one thing" I willingly asked "what". He said "why you praise others in my class I don't like it, you are my mom". I was surprised and willingly accepted the change I needed to save my relation. I said "Yes, but I shall remain your mom always and you are my best friend and best of all". He smiled and smiled and said, "thank you mom". . . . so you know some times we can't overlook small efforts that we need to change, here I got two things learned that my son is very much , concerned for me and second that I need to strengthen my relation more . . .

This small changes are very necessary for the things to work, hence we can try our best to make our near ones dear ones more happy making our bonds intact with no cracks no confusions no misunderstandings and no doubts . . . relations are like water no colour no shape no smell taking shape of container and always need to flow . . .

We need to focus on little things that need a change we can join all the broken strings together again We all are very different from each other someone seek more attention of love care bondings appraisals some are ok feel easy going so you need to understand the very meaning of every relation you are living because all we need a very happy and meaningful life . . .

Keep understanding keep knowing keep making little efforts to be in harmony with the vibrant flow of this beautiful life.

34

Let go—and move on

When we start taking care of our body when we start taking care of our mind we start taking care of the soul that resides in we also indulge in making our soul to rest in a sound body. If we are occupied with burdens of ego pain hurts distress this rising of sound body is not at all possible we need to let go and move forward.

When you think that you can't take some things more you decide to give up and let it go since giving up Means giving up your fears allowing your struggles to limit the opportunities. when we let go we start Freeing our self from something that serves us no longer and gives no meaning further.

Letting go serves like detoxifying yourself from all those things that constantly keep you occupied by giving no reason of its presence that's going to be stagnant and get stale one day. Let go is self liberation you release so many things from your mind from your memories making more space for good things to be accommodated.

Something that is interfering in the growth that is disturbing in the enlighten of the happiness should always be released let it go move forward one step ahead. Remind yourself that you do not need permissions or approvals to be happy it's all in your control to Give up pains release that is hurting you move ahead move forward. We need to start getting more time for ourselves.

Making it a habit to forgive others often and start discarding things you can't accept or that can't be changed just be yourself start taking more care of yourself keep moving with lots of confidence and inner strength. We need to cleanse ourselves from all the grudges just keep on forgiving forgetting releasing the pains and sorrows doing your best deeds and keep moving let go is the best remedy for inner strength if we keep on expecting more and more we will be never satisfied and can't live a more contented life. Thus keep on moving let go things that can't be changed adding more meaning to this life.

KEEP SMILING KEEP MOVING IN LIFE.

35

*Little changes . . . be kind
be humble be courteous—*

When we are in pain when we are hurted when we are going through stressed part of our life no one see much but when you do some mistake you are noticed everywhere. This is hard fact of today s life everyone is quiet busy updating their own spaces we hardly get time to see.

Now days people are overburdened with work with their life styles working habits their schedules relations are just make n break line. Stress levels are elevated everywhere people are becoming more aggressive. Sometimes people do not need advice they just need a heart to listen what they have been piling up since ages. Until they drain all out that has been hurting them inside.

This is the need of the day try being very humble to everyone can bring little change to the one who is already down in his morale. Keep practicing more kindness what it will cost you nothing but what it will earn you is that cannot be measured. On the scales, isn't it. This will be par excellence in the count of humanity when you are more humble more peaceful more easy to approach you will see and feel the effects that brings you magnified results the amount of love care affection you receive in return the environment becomes more enlightened more peaceful.

When you choose to be good in your deeds you get all the good because this leads to more happiness too . . . since you are happy from inside your attitude towards everything remains to be in peace and gratified and this highlights your aura. In more dimensions. it amplifies the purity of your soul it shows on your face too . . . you always seems to be cheerful . . . and feel delighted in small happiness and achievements. Can you imagine what change it brings these small efforts these little changes of your approach add up to change in into broader avenues of more wonderful more amazing truth of life.

We get to understand others more better when we are in peace when we show all our kindness we are in more of our positive outlook and imagine fulfilled but you do your bit in the world soothing there pains not doing but being kind understanding them and the pleasure of being understood to the person who thinks his quench of being understood is fulfilled . . . .

This enhances our personality too when you be more peaceful more kind more humble your social attitude your social behavior makes difference you get blessings love affection and you are surrounded by more of positivity . . . this makes a greater meaning to this life . . . . so keep inspiring keep being humble keep doing good keep on smiling feel the good . . . .

36

Willingly learn from all

Our family our dear ones our friends our close associates whom we are close know us quiet well. Since we have close bonding to each other they are well aware of our strength weakness flaws our potentials our awards and so they are even used to our way our habits.

We must seek open comments if they try to find some kind of fault some mistakes we do or they assess you finding you to be more accurate. We should welcome such gestures as this are the way we can know more of our flaws we know whenever we need corrections we should not be ashamed with such comments we fear we lose our pride we lose our respect if they observe and correct us. We may be using to retaliate to such comments as self defencing mechanism but the fact remains the same we do not know ourselves more we need a mirror for our image so our friends our family help us as they act like a mirror to rectify the little flaws we need to work on.

We also need to openly welcome and start taking initiatives to correct the spotted flaws with in you. Try to be accepting more open comments suggestions add this to your goodwill this is short cut for your Growth from inside you become more matured more practical . . . more reasonable to understand the things associated with you in your life.

With all your courage and humbleness let you drop your ego and stand to be corrected often agree to the understanding and observations by your friends and family. Try to learn more from all your friends they are helping you to understand more of you do some times ask them for their advice this make them more special. they will be more happy to make you even better. You become more humble reflecting on your personality adding one more feather to the cap that you are willingly accepting your flaws and also rectifying them isn't this more commandable.

Whatever is discussed or the exchange of thoughts are between you and the known person to you so no need to feel ashamed or depressed just keep learning everyday more you learn from your mistakes more you learn from your flaws more you become crafted and smooth in your life there is no chance that you get wrong feedbacks this are the feed backs from your own friends and family they make you grow so always be willing to accept your flaws your report card, make them shine and shine always, so keep understanding keep learning keep smiling and add more meaning to your life.

37

Write down your habits good bad —work on them

The more we are aware the more we are peaceful the more we are responsible to our achievement to our goals to be patient to be more humble to be more kind is a quality and the supreme way to go. The more peace you are the more you are ready to accept the hardest realities of life. Life is the way you want it to be for you . . . without being at peace we can't stand to be strong getting annoyed getting angry impulsive is all signs of restless soul which is not at peace This becomes our habit, this unbalancing acts ruins our life to a very great extent all that is faced we get pains and hardest to survive.

We should be aware of our good and bad habits. We can work on our flaws very effectively. We can enhance our good habits more we can add more to this. Similarly we should be quiet aware of our bad habits too. We can write down all our stubborn habits that irritates others, thus making some little effort towards. More progressive approach to our life.

We can write all the good points that make us happy and all the bad points that make us sad. We must be always ready to rectify our drawbacks to achieve success we can just maintain our good habits improving more on them this will in return add up for more positive changes.

When you start writing down perhaphs you will be aware that where you need to be rectified. Which habits are broken you and are actually not essential and that are making waste in your life. Just if you sleep more just try to rectify this can be achieved. It takes a lot of patience and self determination to quit your habits. But once you highlight your flaws and your good points in life it becomes very easy to really know where you are heading in life which part of your life holds you in stronger lines. If for instance some one likes more to write this can be added as your hidden potential and you can actually make down yourself into writing. Thus all that are your plus points or that things you wish can add up you to flourish and make you happy just start pursuing. Keep going, keep smiling.

38

Rejuvenate revive yourself

It is very essential to care for yourself not only for yourself but to get transformed to get all the inner strength to get inner peace and contentment. To rejuvenate yourself all again . . . When we filter our emotions we become more stronger and are prepared for our life. When we set in inner peace we incorporate more of ourselves when we inhibit the magic of relaxation.

We perfectly settle our drilled brains into more peace once more energizing it for better accumulation of peaceful life . . . the finess creation of our divine god is human brain—it's our honour to be in this life we need to care our body soul . . . our mind need peace relaxation we need to rejuvenate our souls. We can practice. On the weekends do what makes you more peaceful. Let us also give break to our minds peace to our minds be quiet for some times then getting the experience of enlightening within ourselves just be calm alone for some time. Listen to your favourite music, go along the beaches just view sun rise and sunsets this all are key to relaxations and make you serene more happy and more peaceful. Is it not more wonderful then actually gossiping and filling our thoughts with unwanted tensions and problems.

Take initiatives to make a rule to give a break to your minds your brains also in weekends. Practice meditation, long walks deep breathing strolling in garden watching trees greenery walking along beaches keeping more near water. Listening birds chirping. Just get the experience, its magical it will rejuvenate you from within you are relaxed and revived with all the inner peace.

We got to be happy from within try to be more calm and get the magic revived of life again, keep reviving keep feeling more pleasant and live this life . . .

Keep doing more that makes you going start your own world of likes and dislikes work on your negative aspects and turn them into positivity.

Just take some time for yourself and try to live this wonderful life keep smiling.

39

Truth may be different—seek it and understand . . .

We all are different individuals we all are raised in different environments we definitely belong to human race but our views our concepts our focuses may be different our tolerance scale our acceptance level may be different That's the truth we need to accept this rather than expecting others to follow and consider your opinions to be right always, seek the truth behind everything that happens the truth may sometime force us to understand that some people strongly take in huge amount of pains inside still maintain a smile on the faces.

Each individual has their own visualization towards words statements opinions or even advice some may like some may not why not to accept the fact all can't be same indeed we all carry different genes different role of brain dynamics are different dimensions are different outlook preview all is different every one follows different mental strategies.

When we are seeking truth behind certain things going right or left we need to consider other factors too that every individual is different when we actually understand to why certain person hold some different opinion we may perhaps eliminate many quarrels that remain unsettled unseen gone misunderstood.

Each one adopts a different way each one responds in a different way each one caters in a different way ever one has different capabilities to cater the things and different way to see face react to an situation this is the truth.

We got to accept and give time whenever we seek a solution rather being more impulsive calmly understand the respective facts we can wait for others to look over the problem when we start understanding work in on their way of dealing problems respecting the line of being human start giving space that individual is seeking getting hold the grain of truth that we need space and we should give space to all others to have a positive move add substantial meaning to this life in more peaceful truth seeking way spacing them to stand where they deserve and not tempting them to make forcibly accept you. we keep inspiring keep smiling keep growing as perfect individuals.

40

---

*Make best of you . . .
get accepted more . . .*

When life puts you in troubles tough situation just happily accept and say yes 'try me' And not 'why me'

Try build more of trust with yourself trust building mechanism makes more of you and you are accepted more . . . a life or situation is effect less until you react. Make all the best in you to cater all those tricky time, be A voice and not an echo. We can grow every day that is mandatory but no where it is written to grow old that still remains optional start living like a child care free enjoying life letting go whatever hurted in two minutes children just forget that some of their friends pushed them or made them cry. feel the innocence and enjoy the very meaning of this life.

We get this life we live once why we take everything for granted can't we respect the lines of humanity and start caring loving one and all. Anything un attended gets rusted tiered off some relation are given to us from god our parents some of the relation we make voluntarily then how can we choose the wrong ones just be in the understanding that you need to take care of each and every relation you got and that you made try your best to nurture them take care but sometimes things do not work then too be nice do not stretch the relations with no meaning that of no use. Just move on get yourself more of peace let go move on make the best efforts ever. Feelings should come from heart you can' t just forcibly let someone to be with you, the line of understanding washes off here if it's not taken from heart, we seek to maintain the flow for ever, we care respect. We willingly accept and get accepted even with our flaws if someone really loves and care.

A life without any purpose is effect less be a voice to your relation do not make it turn into screams, that's meaningless Be pleasant get accepted let your persona accomplish you more and your loved ones seek you the way you are get yourself understand more when we understand the values of our relations we care but sometimes it's too late.

Because time never stays at one place lots of time we waste in ego clashes agreeing disagreeing not getting to know each other but if we feel for one other from heart care more get to know more of each other we can love and nurture our relationship into never breaking bond. Thus adding more meaning to be in this life keep getting knowing each other more keep smiling keep moving.

41

Its habit that makes most of you

If you spread love you get it back as love if you spread hate you get it back as hate that is eternal law What you sow so you reap. Thus what you practice more what you show up more, you become that If I indulge more of myself in any activity I am habituated to again and again it starts reflecting more in me, thus if you want love start spreading more of love it goes that simple, start giving that what you want of others do for you.

If you are stubborn full of hate lots of hate comes back to you arising in each segment of life and love grows more with enthusiasm and prosper more. Thus all the sweetness calmness peace we can't buy with all the bank balance. This are all born with our karmas that we do and that we display.

Never hence display your attitude just spread more of peace more of joy more of care. What you project that will be displayed in front. Don't expect more, just keep doing your best deeds. Do the righteous act don't walk on shortcuts, but try a tougher path we get more to learn here. Do not discriminate just do what is good and that makes you more comfortable and happy. If you start getting annoyed for small issues for small things that may inculcated as your habit further adding in to your personality into more of negative behavior and full of attitude arrogance and making you rude. The more you are positive the more you are humble more dignified you feel from right inside your heart. You don't feel hurted you get more mature to forgive who hurts you.

You become more of what you practice to be if you choose to be cheerful more kind more humble You are more motivated to be that because habit keeps you moving more in positive outlooks of life; Here there are no fears its truth of your inner self subsiding all over pure thoughts making you pure Enhancing your persona your magnified aura that makes you feel special from inside and that keeps you Always in joyful condition. More binding into being human for what we are here supposed to be more graceful more gratified behavior adding up more of meaning to this wonderful elegant vibrant life.

keep smiling keep making best of your habits.

42

Do that which make you happy the most

Being in this life is just very much wonderful feel privileged to be in here. Start putting little more efforts to do something that keeps you going. If you are unaware start exploring the one little thing that keeps you going.

Since when you know what makes you more happy and really happy that thing keeps you motivated always use it as your asset. Save some good moments for yourself too. This enlightens you from inside giving immense pleasure happiness motivating thrust to live more because you start looking life as wonderful amazing gift. Take time from your schedule let it be even 15 minutes go for a walk if you feel that relaxes you. Go for walking in a garden, watch the nature listen your favourite music or take up your special subject to read once a week call your friends make some weekend programmes take up gardening there are many things that keep you motivated specially which you love from your heart and that makes you happy contented goes well just take paints and start painting on canvas, it's just initiative take some little step and start changing your routines enhancing more of your inner beings, inner strength . . . your soul starts energizing new avenues of more peace more happiness more glad in different perspective toward's life and start re living once again to the fullest adding more meaning to your life . . . . keep smiling keep moving keep exploring your inner self keep yourself happy.

43

Every minute you are angry you lose sixty seconds of happiness

If I am disappointed today, I try to kill my today unknowingly, and that this day is lost, I overshadow my today and tomorrow also.

With darkness I lose foresight of new dreams that could arise tomorrow every second is countable in this life. sometimes this seconds do count. we get to know from sports person each second what it means to them. they get awarded even with fraction of second makes a great difference same is applicable in our life every second add to a minute we lose 60 seconds of happiness just calculate how many seconds we must have wasted from the time we are born. when we want to know the value of minutes days years just see the old woman still waiting from years for her son to come from the war calculate the time when a desperate mother seeking birth of her children waiting for nine months in her womb Caring and nurturing her baby.

Every second is very important every second can make a difference every minute you get angry you lose so many good things that could have happened in that one minute We just can't let it go we start to invest in love selfcare indulging into good habits utilizing every minute every moment into more progressive activity nothing comes without reason all that is destined comes at proper time we just can't sit on the ground waiting we need to put efforts by ourself every minute adds up to make a bigger difference everyday life changes we get some bad some hard times some times easy I love to live today this moment with joy what is today may not be tomorrow.

It's the today that matters more it's the happiness that matters more why to waste all our life just we need to understand that we need to get contented with what we have and make best of ourself and make life better keep smiling keep moving keep understanding the meaning of every second every minute every hour every day every week every season all has to be in the place for a reason. We can't just get angry we should seek the reasons we should be more careful, expressing and understanding is very essential. If we just get angry for small issues we add more to negativity. When we are angry we often try to ruin our own health but when we try to be happy we add up to our health some beautiful moments. Stop getting angry just start being more happy more cheerful.

44

---

*Make your valuable experiences gift
for your children*

We continuously strive very hard the entire life to achieve success we are surged into tremendous ups and downs of life we all acquire what we need through all the phases of life we all go through different environments into the phases we got different experience to all these . . .

We all are well prepared for all even the toughest one. similarly each day we get to learn more the more we learn the more we grow we get more wise with our experiences. I personally feel everyone should follow the habit of writing in there valuable experiences and treasuring the gift to their children and grand children. Try to write down in a book what were your struggles in life how did you get to manage to move this can be great help motivation lessons for your coming generations, they will be fortunate to read all that understanding your efforts how you made your dreams into your destiny, i am sure this can do wonders.

They will be obliged to learn from your experiences your teachings this way you will be making them more aware to your old cultures and traditions too which now a days are getting to be vanished . . . is it not this more resourceful way to re construct your roots again in a very different way . . . They will understand how difficult was at your times to go through the things and how easy they get everything today just by a click of a button . . . this may also inculcate more values more respect and more understanding in between the generations. This enormous exchange of thoughts your hardships your achievements when displayed for your children in form of some manuscripts or book may inspire them a lot and surely going to be helpful.

It requires deep and immense practice to know oneself more. when you share your experiences the words may speak like rocks may target softly but sure to impact them . . . The expansion of our life experiences also gives you a great satisfaction that you did a bit for your children for the society for a good cause you tried to explain different shades of life making meaningful approach to others to make simple attempt that can result immensely.

A mind when dealing with different experiences achieving new heights new experiences can never set back and fit in same dimensions from where he managed to take a leap . . . when you understand all the suffering could not been avoided but definitely they must have managed to give you some glory some kind of satisfaction. That matters a lot. The pain that you have been gone through life may be soothing when you try to explain it with how you managed to come out of it this weakness becomes your strength to climb into greater heights, aiming high . . . just don't let shadows of yesterday cast shadow on your today . . . start reviving yourself more with all your achievements being happy to share re living all the phases of life to the fullest . . . leaping forward your destiny.

Thus making more desirable happiness that you deserve and adding more meaning to your life . . . keep smiling keep inspiringkeep moving keep living in this wonderful life . . .

45

Life is a gift . . . . live it

Start your morning with a heart filled with gratitude towards god for giving you one another day to live in.

This day is been gifted to you to explore more of your potentials to search for more opportunities . . . life is indeed very precious we can't afford to waste it. This life has more to say more to express try to understand the innocence of others. Be polite, be a good listener and see the magic of what you say what you hear and what you got to understand. Just be yourself and do all that is good and see the almighty blessing you as never before he knows all your pain he knows how much you can bear . . . that's life we got to live with it be thankful to god if we start disliking this life god also starts testing us more harder . . . if we are happy with whatever is stored for us we get unbelievable amount of just happiness.

Try to be cheerful often start getting to know yourself more and understand others more. When we know ourselves more we know where to start where we are comfortable and where we can't hold ourselves we can take proper precautions well in hand before. We are well prepared for all the surprises as we are more in good knowledge and more in wisdom we get to understand the circumstances better . . . we are able to judge know seek solutions better.

Make a place for yourself also give others the place they deserve we need to respect in the lines where we are act more humanly . . . we need to really know the power of being humble. do most which makes you happy when we are happy from inside we live the life and make our surrounding a better place.

Do not ignore your health keep track of your eating habits. drink lots of water practice deep breathing practice meditation this all de toxifies your entire body and you emerge out as pure soul who knows to be humble who knows how to live a soul who knows the actual purpose of being here . . . why we are in human race this is very important aspect to be understood we could have been anything from a fish a bird or even an animal but god chosen us to give this life isn't it more than enough to love this life as a gift and acknowledge this being thankful for all.

Get yourself more organized read good books stay away from all those things that make you unhappy or that serve no reason to be in you r life. Life means to move on constantly growing each day with your wisdom acquiring all good thoughts and spreading love, making this world a better place to live in.

Start exploring different colours hidden in life I sincerely wish everyone to love this life immensely enjoy this life it is very, very beautiful we are the ones who make it good or bad . . . we should be obliged to be in this life . . . be thankful to god for bestowing innumerable blessings each day live a cheerful life;

Sometimes you have to forget what is gone and just appreciate what you have. Life is balance of holding and letting go. In both situations you have to cater about holding how you move ahead with your head up with no regrets and taking life a pleasant journey and letting go that can't be changed keep moving in life keep smiling be happy always. Love this life and add more meaning to your life.

take care . . . .